Meet
Thomas Jefferson

In Congress, July 4, 1776

The unanimous Declaration of the thirteen united States of Am

PHILOSOPHY

NATURAL HISTORY

POETRY

Louisiana Purchase

University of Virginia

Meet
Thomas
Jefferson

Written by Patricia A. Pingry
Illustrated by Meredith Johnson

ideals children's books™
Nashville, Tennessee

ISBN 0-8249-5459-9

Published by Ideals Children's Books
An imprint of Ideals Publications
A division of Guideposts
535 Metroplex Drive, Suite 250
Nashville, Tennessee 37211
www.idealsbooks.com

Printed and bound in Mexico by RR Donnelley

Library of Congress Cataloging-in-Publication Data
Pingry, Patricia A.,
Meet Thomas Jefferson / by Patricia A. Pingry ; illustrated by
Meredith Johnson.
    p. cm.
Summary: An introduction to the life of the statesman who wrote the
Declaration of Independence and became the third president of the United
States.
    ISBN 0-8249-5459-0 (alk. paper)
    1. Jefferson, Thomas, 1743-1826--Juvenile literature. 2.
Presidents--United States--Biography--Juvenile literature. [1. Jefferson,
Thomas, 1743-1826. 2. Presidents.] I. Johnson, Meredith, ill. II. Title.
    E332.79 . P56 2002
    973.4'6'092--dc21
                            2002015027

10 9 8 7 6 5 4 3 2 1

Our thanks go to Dorothy Twohig, Ph.D., Editor-in-Chief Emeritus,
The Papers of George Washington, University of Virginia,
for reading and commenting on this manuscript.

For Abigail

I cannot live without books.

Determine never to be idle.

It is wonderful how much may be done if we are always doing.

We hold these truths to be self-evident; that all men are created equal;
that they are endowed by their Creator with certain unalienable Rights;
that among these are Life, Liberty, and the pursuit of Happiness. . . .

—Thomas Jefferson

Nine-year-old Thomas Jefferson closed his book and leaned back against the tree as the sun slid behind Virginia's Blue Ridge Mountains. Thomas had been born right here at Shadwell on April 13, 1743, and he didn't think there was any place in the world as beautiful as Virginia in the spring.

Thomas peered through the haze for a glimpse of the little mountain across the river. He dreamed that someday he would build a house on that mountaintop. He would plant flower gardens and fruit trees, and he

would grow his own vegetables. Every morning he would ride his horse around his mountaintop. Someday . . .

"**Thomas,**" called his sister Jane. "**Father's home!**"

Thomas picked up his book and raced back to the house.

"Father," he called as he burst into the door. "Have you finished your work in the wilderness?"

"I have so much to tell you," replied Peter Jefferson, putting out his arms for his son. "We ran into swamps and lost some of our horses. But we completed the survey. Now all of Virginia is mapped for the king."

Peter Jefferson was a surveyor who was often away from home. Thomas missed his father when he was gone, but Thomas was never lonely. He had a large family and his father's library of forty books. Thomas had read them all at least once.

When Thomas was very young, he was tutored at home. But now, Thomas left home during the school year and stayed with the family of the schoolmaster, Reverend William Douglas.

The next morning, Thomas saddled his pony and began the fourteen-mile ride back to the small school. There were only five boys in his class and no girls or servants.

One of the boys, Dabney Carr, called to Thomas one day, **"Let's have a race and see if your pony can beat my horse."**

Thomas knew that his pony could not beat Dabney's horse but he didn't intend to be beaten. So Thomas said, **"I'll race you on February 30."** Thomas fooled Dabney. February never has thirty days!

When Thomas was fourteen years old, his father died. Thomas now owned the home at Shadwell and the bookcase of forty books. He also owned the small mountain across the river and twenty-two slaves, or servants, as Thomas called them.

Thomas now went to school closer to Shadwell. Every weekend, he returned home to help his mother with the other children, especially with the twins who were only two

years old. At home, Thomas went on long walks with his oldest sister, Jane. They collected leaves, bark, insects, rocks, flowers, and seeds and took them home to study. In the evenings he played his violin while Jane sang.

When Thomas was seventeen, he entered the College of William and Mary. He was six feet, two inches tall with big feet and hands, and he pulled his red hair back in a ponytail. In the summertime, his face was covered with freckles.

Thomas studied fifteen hours *every day*! Then he practiced his violin for three hours. After Thomas graduated from college, he studied the law; and at the age of twenty-four, he began the practice of law in Albermarle County, Virginia.

In 1768, Thomas was elected to the Virginia House of Burgesses. There was no United States then, only thirteen colonies owned by England. Thomas tried to pass a law that made it easier to free slaves, but the other Burgesses rejected that idea. They wanted to talk about England and the taxes they took from Virginians. They talked of the coming war with England.

While the colonies planned for war, Thomas planned his home on top of the mountain. He named the mountain *Monticello* which means "little mountain" in Italian. Thomas searched for books about architecture. He designed his house and drew up plans. He planted fruit trees and began to build.

In 1770, while Thomas was away, his home at Shadwell caught fire and burned to the ground. When the servant told him about the fire, Thomas asked, **"Did you save my books and my notes?"**

The answer came, **"No, nothing was saved."**

So Thomas moved to Monticello.

One day Thomas met a young widow named Martha Wayles Skelton. The liked to play musical duets, she on the piano and he on his violin.

She and Thomas fell in love and were married January 1, 1772. After the wedding they left for Monticello.

Thomas and Martha had two daughters they named Martha and Mary, but Thomas called them Patsy and Polly.

Thomas built a bigger house. He and his servants planted more gardens and fruit trees. They made beautiful furniture. Thomas bought more and more books for his library. Thomas was very happy.

In 1775, war broke out between the American colonies and England. Thomas was appointed delegate to the Second Continental Congress that met in Philadelphia. Because Thomas was the best writer of the group, he was asked to write a declaration to the king of England.

Thomas wrote that the thirteen colonies were independent of England. He said **"all men are created equal"** and have the right to freedom.

On July 4, 1776, Congress approved the Declaration of Independence. Throughout the thirteen colonies, the declaration was read to the people, and the people cheered. Thomas's words were some of the most important words ever written.

In 1784, Thomas was sent to France as minister for the United States. Martha had died, so he took his daughter Patsy with him. Thomas admired the French architecture, furniture, and cooking. He even sent his servant to a French cooking school. When Thomas came home, President Washington appointed him Secretary of State.

In 1796 Thomas became vice president, and in 1800 the people elected Thomas the third president of the United States. He was the first president to be inaugurated in the new capital of Washington, D.C.

In 1803, France wanted to sell five hundred million acres of land called the Lousiana Territory. It was a bargain at only fifteen million dollars! When Thomas bought the land for the United States, he doubled the size of the country.

Thomas asked Meriwether Lewis to lead the Corps of Discovery to explore the new land. They returned with maps of the wilderness, drawings of animals, plants, and birds never seen before, and information about the Native American tribes they met. Thomas placed their maps and gifts in Monticello.

In 1804 Thomas was re-elected president, but four years later it was time for him to go home. He saddled his horse and rode through a snowstorm back to Monticello, to his library, and to his family. Thomas was glad to be back on his mountaintop.

Now Thomas lived like a farmer. He wore corduroy trousers and riding boots. He got up with the sun and rode his horse Eagle around his land. He walked through the woods every day. He wrote letters and kept records of his seeds. He designed more gardens and helped the servants prune the roses. He invented a plow for the side of the mountain and a bookstand

so he could read five books at a time. He organized races for his grandchildren. He tore down Monticello and had his servants build it up again. And he bought more and more books.

People came from all over the world to see the author of the
Declaration of Independence. Sometimes as many as fifty people
stayed overnight. Sometimes Thomas didn't even know who the
people were.

In 1814 the United States was at war with England again. English troops burned Washington, D.C., and the federal library. So Thomas sold his library to the government. His 7,000 books were loaded onto ten wagons and pulled by oxen down the mountain. Thomas's books started the Library of Congress.

But Thomas couldn't stand looking at his empty book shelves. **"I cannot live without books,"** he said. So he bought more books.

When Thomas was seventy-six, he had an idea that would help young people. His idea became the University of Virginia. Thomas designed the campus, helped select the teachers, and chose the books for the library.

On clear days, Thomas stood on his mountaintop and watched the construction of the university in the valley below.

July 4, 1826, was the fiftieth anniversary of the Declaration of Independence. That afternoon, Thomas died at Monticello. He was eighty-six years old.

Thomas was president, inventor, architect, and builder. He built

Monticello and the University of Virginia. His books laid the foundation for

the Library of Congress, and his Louisiana Purchase built a larger country.

But most of all, his words in the Declaration of Independence still inspire all

of us to build a world where **"all men are created equal."**